THE
WATER
REALM

Pastor Uzor Ndekwu

THE
WATER
REALM

Pastor Uzor Ndekwu

MEMOIRS
Cirencester

United Kingdom:

Uzor Ndekwu Ministries (Jesus Sanctuary)
25/27 Ruby Street
Old Kent Road
London SE15 1LR
United Kingdom
Tel: +44 207 277 5664; +44 7961 276 187
Email: info@jesussanctuaryministries.org
Website: www.jesussanctuaryministries.org

Nigeria:

Uzor Ndekwu Ministries (Jesus Sanctuary)
41 Otigba Crescent
GRA
Onitsha
Anambra State
Nigeria
Te: +234 803 395 0197; +234 803 405 2113

Published by:

Uzor Ndekwu Ministries (Jesus Sanctuary)

Bible quotations are from the King James Version of the Holy Bible.

Printed by

Memoirs Publishers
England

ISBN 978-1-908223-67-8

THE
WATER REALM

CONTENTS:	Page

ACKNOWLEDGEMENTS

I wish to express my profound thanks to the following persons: my wife for her help and support and for checking and editing the original draft, Pastor Obi (Pastor of Jesus Sanctuary Ministries, Onitsha Branch) for the insightful testimonies, Dr Osakwe Chinweuba (the former occultist who gave his life to Christ and is now a Minister of God) for his powerful insights into the activities of occultic people using the water, Brother Andrew Onwuemene, who typed the original manuscript and Mr Chris Newton for the editing and proof-reading of the book.

CHAPTER 1 - INTRODUCTION

Spiritually, very little is known about the waters or sea realm. There are few literatures on the origin of creation of the waters. Even the scriptures did not expressly state much about the origin of water. The scripture introduced the waters as a given or existing entity which harboured the Spirit of God right before God began His creative activities.

> *"And the Spirit of God moved upon the face of the waters. And God said, Let there be light: and there was light."* (Genesis 1:2-3).

From the above scriptures, it is clear that the water realm was just introduced as an existing entity, which provided a platform on which the Spirit of God operated during the season of creation.

Water is mentioned again in the scripture when God decided to divide the firmament from the waters.

"And God said, Let there be a firmament in the midst of the waters, and let it divide the waters from the waters. And God made the firmament, and divided the waters which were under the firmament from the waters which were above the firmament: and it was so. And God called the firmament Heaven..." (Genesis 1:6-8).

It is necessary to understand that the dividing of the waters from the waters does not imply a physical partition or separation, but a sort of interconnection between the waters that are held up in the clouds and those that are gathered on the earth as sea.

The scripture once again mentioned water when God wanted the earth to appear from the womb of the waters:

"And God said, Let the waters under the heaven be gathered together unto one place, and let the dry land appear: and it was so. And God called the dry land

Earth; and the gathering together of the waters called he Seas" (Genesis 1:9-10).

From this biblical account, it is obvious that God called the gathering of the waters as seas. No mention was made of how in the beginning God created water. As the scripture clearly stated for heaven and earth –

"In the beginning God created the heaven and the earth." (Genesis 1:1).

What is indisputable is that there was a time the waters were pregnant with the earth. So when the pregnancy was due according to God's timetable, the womb of the waters delivered the "baby earth" through the process of commandment.

There is therefore a sort of mother-child relationship and bond between the waters and the earth, just as there is a strong bond and an unending attachment between mother and child. The earth depends endlessly on the water for her nourishment and resourcefulness. Before the earth can be utilized for anything, be it agricultural, structural or domestic (gardening), water as an element must be introduced.

When God decided to create man, He first of all caused it to rain upon the face of the earth:

> *"And every plant of the field before it was in the earth, and every herb of the field before it grew: for the LORD God had not caused it to rain upon the earth, and there was not a man to till the ground. But there went up a mist from the earth, and watered the whole face of the ground. And the LORD God formed man of the dust of the ground, and breathed into his nostrils the breath of life; and man became a living soul."* *(Genesis 2:5-7).*

The water therefore is like the milk that brings out the best of the earth, just as good motherhood brings out the best in a child.

On the other hand, the waters can be used to discipline or stamp out what is not good for the earth. When man sinned and the earth became full of wickedness, God used water to destroy the earth. According to the scriptures:

"And the LORD said, I will destroy man whom I have created from the face of the earth; both man, and beast, and the creeping thing, and the fowls of the air; for it repenteth me that I have made them." (Genesis 6:7)

and

"For yet seven days, and I will cause it to rain upon the earth forty days and forty nights; and every living substance that I have made will I destroy from off the face of the earth." (Genesis 7:4).

The ceaseless rain for seven days that we call Noah's flood was used by God to destroy the wicked earth and begin a fresh start with mankind and other creatures. The spiritual superiority of the water over the earth is underscored by this incidence in Biblical times. Even in our present age and technological advancement, water in the form of floods has devastated some states and communities. The tsunamis and the tropical storms in Japan, Thailand, Pakistan, India, Russia, the USA and China demonstrate the power of water over the earth.

The waters' role in the season of creation manifested itself when God commanded the moving and living creatures to come out of the waters:

"And God said, Let the waters bring forth abundantly the moving creature that hath life, and fowl that may fly above the earth in the open firmament of heaven. And God created great whales, and every living creature that moveth, which the waters brought forth abundantly, after their kind, and every winged fowl after his kind: and God saw that it was good." (Genesis 1:20-21).

From this encounter, the spiritual dynamics of water as a realm in its highest form were revealed. The response of water to the commands of God showed that the water realm is a living entity. All through the history of creation, the power of command was demonstrated by God. Invariably, we who are made in the image of God and after His likeness have also the ability to command creation. Creation should never be worshipped. All we need to do is command it for our desired goals.

CHAPTER 2
THE POWER OF COMMAND

Indeed when the scripture says:

> *"Thus saith the LORD, the Holy One of Israel, and his Maker, ask me of things to come concerning my sons, and concerning the work of my hands command ye me."* (Isaiah 45:11),

the scripture is in no way encouraging us to command God, because man cannot instruct his maker. The actual meaning of this is that man can command God through His creative works. For, indeed, creation itself is a product of command:

> *"Let them praise the name of the LORD: for he commanded, and they were created."* (Psalms 148:5).

In fact, God's first statement to Adam was by command:

"And the LORD God commanded the man, saying, Of every tree of the garden thou mayest freely eat:" (Genesis 2:16).

It could therefore be seen that in the realm of the spirit, commandment is a mode of communication, while in the realm of the physical, it is dialogue and consensus.

All through the scriptures, the servants of God, from Moses to Malachi, often begin their prophetic utterances with *"Thus saith the Lord"* or *"And the Lord commanded"*. It is equally important to note that in the encounter between Satan and Jesus Christ in the wilderness, the scripture recorded that:

"And when the tempter came to him, he said, If thou be the Son of God, command that these stones be made bread." (Matthew 4:3).

It shows that even Satan knew that the language of the spirit is based on command. That is why he asked Jesus Christ to command the stones to be made bread.

We ought to give commands to situations or circumstances we want to change or influence. This is because commanding words carry the aura of authority and power. And authority and power are the currency of the spirit realm. For example, in your dream state there are things you can be commanded to do in the dream, like eating or making love, which in the physical realm you would not agree to do.

No wonder the Lord queried Job:

> *"Hast thou commanded the morning since thy days; and caused the dayspring to know his place?" (Job 38:12).*

God was reminding Job about the spiritual basics of utilising the currency of command to make his day work in his favour. Those that understand the prophetic always speak to the powers of the morning to respond to their desired goals for that day, for the morning holds the key of the day. Furthermore, the blessings of the day are renewed every morning, which therefore makes it vital for us to make a demand on the covenant blessings of the day by using the Word of God to decree to the morning.

The scripture says in Job 22:28: *"Thou shalt also decree a thing, and it shall be established unto thee: and the light shall shine upon thy ways."*. To decree means to command. Our Lord Jesus Christ used the power of commandment to instruct both the visible and the invisible forces:

> *"And they were all amazed, insomuch that they questioned among themselves, saying, What thing is this? what new doctrine is this? for with authority commandeth he even the unclean spirits, and they do obey him." (Mark 1:27).*

And the scripture even says the wind and the sea responded to the command of Jesus Christ:

> *"And he said unto them, Where is your faith? And they being afraid wondered, saying one to another, What manner of man is this! for he commandeth even the winds and water, and they obey him."*
> *(Luke 8:25).*

Just like Jesus Christ, those who have the understanding that creation can be commanded to utilise the services of these realms (heaven, earth, and water) for their own purpose, as earlier mentioned. However, among these realms, though they were all created by God and with shared characteristics of His creative nature, the water realm has some distinguishing features and dynamics which are unique and powerful.

First, the water realm is the most spiritualized. This is because the Spirit of God has been on the face of the waters before the heavens and the earth were separated from the waters (see Genesis 1:1-10). The waters served as a platform to the creative activities of God, which conferred on her (the water) the "motherhood" of other realms. Furthermore, the waters have a sort of sovereign status, which makes her independent of man. They are not subject to man's rulership. Man was only permitted to dominate the fish of the sea:

> *"…and let them have dominion over the fish of the sea." (Genesis 1:26)*

which limited man's ability to control the powers and authorities of the waters. Unlike the waters, the scripture says that God has given man the earth, and the heavens are for the Lord (Psalms 115:16). The water being the platform of the creative activities of God and its independent status, they are the most spiritualized, and the most sensitive to instructions and commands.

Water has always been the first contact in the realm of the miraculous. When God wanted to deal with the wickedness of man on earth, water was used as an instrument of judgement (Genesis 6:13-17). Moses' first plague against the Egyptians has to do with water which became rivers of blood all over Egypt (Exodus 7:20-21). Jesus Christ's first miracle was to turn the six water pots of stone into sweet wine during a marriage ceremony (John 2:6-9). The Psalmist thanked God for drawing him out of many waters (Psalm 18:16), while Job asked for the abundance of waters (blessings) (Job 38:34). Believers' bellies are to release rivers of living water (John 7:38).

Secondly, the waters' formidability is based on the mutual connection and relationship between the heavens and the earth. Although the firmament was used to separate the waters from the heavens, the partition was physical, as I mentioned earlier, not spiritual. The water is linked to the heavens through the firmament (cloud) and the heavens are the domain of the wicked forces. According to the scriptures:

> *"For we wrestle not against flesh and blood, but against principalities, against powers, against the rulers of the darkness of this world, against spiritual wickedness in high places."*
> *(Ephesians 6:12).*

These high places are in the firmament of heavens, which is linked with the water. And between the water and the heavens, there is the wind element which serves as the passage link for demonic connections and activities between the heavens and the water realms. As Prophet Daniel noted:

> *"...I saw in my vision by night, and, behold, the four winds of the heaven strove upon the great sea. And four great*

beasts came up from the sea, diverse one from another." (Daniel 7:2-3).

So, the wind, which is the air in motion, is a powerful element in relationship to the waters. What water is to the earth is what the air or wind is to the waters. The course of action the water or sea takes is dependent on the air movement or direction. As the scripture says

"And the sea arose by reason of a great wind that blew." (John 6:18).

When Jesus Christ wanted to calm the sea,

"...he arose, and rebuked the wind, and said unto the sea, Peace, be still. And the wind ceased, and there was a great calm." (Mark 4:39).

It is instructive to note that Jesus Christ did not rebuke the sea that was troubling. He spoke to the wind instead. Jesus knew that there is a link between the wind and the waters and that powers, principalities and authorities in high places operate through the wind. The movement of the waters is dependent solely on the course of direction the wind takes. And there are different types of winds; namely: the East, West, South and North winds. Generally, the wind is a powerful force of nature, and man has utilized its energy to harness power for electricity.

In spiritual matters, the wind in conjunction with the water realm, is a powerful instrument. For example, Prophet Moses used the east wind to divide the Red Sea and deliverance came to the Israelites:

> *"And Moses stretched out his hand over the sea; and the LORD caused the sea to go back by a strong East wind all that night..." (Exodus 14:21).*

The same Prophet Moses

> *"...stretched forth his hand over the sea, and the sea returned to his strength...... and the LORD overthrew the Egyptians in the midst of the sea." (Exodus 14:27).*

The west wind was used by the Lord to drive

'spiritual' locusts into the Red Sea. The locusts represent oppressors and devourers of our blessings (Exodus 10:19). The north wind takes away rain (Proverbs 25:23), and the south wind is the promoter of quietness on the earth (Job 37:17). The waters and wind complement each other, and that connection gives the powers and authorities in the water unusual demonic strength. That explains why the water realm is the most powerful among all the realms.

Furthermore, the existence of Behemoth and Leviathan creatures in the waters solidified the strongholds of Satan in the waters. As earlier mentioned, man was given power only to dominate the fish kingdom (Genesis 1:26). When man sinned, Satan took over the fish kingdom, and that gave him opportunity for demonic possession of the whale and crocodile-like fishes. These creatures became symbols of Satan in the waters. As said by Isaiah,

> *"In that day the LORD with his sore and great and strong sword shall punish leviathan the piercing serpent, even*

leviathan that crooked serpent; and he shall slay the dragon that is in the sea." (Isaiah 27:1).

And Job did mention the existence of these creatures:

"Behold now behemoth, which I made with thee; he eateth grass as an ox. Lo now, his strength is in his loins, and his force is in the navel of his belly. He moveth his tail like a cedar: the sinews of his stones are wrapped together. His bones are as strong pieces of brass; his bones are like bars of iron. He is the chief of the ways of God: he that made him can make his sword to approach unto him. Surely the mountains bring him forth food, where all the beasts of the field play. He lieth under the shady trees, in the covert of the reed, and fens. The shady trees cover him with their shadow; the willows of the brook compass him about. Behold, he drinketh up a river, and hasteth not: he trusteth that he can draw

up Jordan into his mouth. He taketh it with his eyes: his nose pierceth through snares. (Job 40:15-24)

and:

"Canst thou draw out leviathan with an hook? or his tongue with a cord which thou lettest down... His scales are his pride, shut up together as with a close seal. One is so near to another, that no air can come between them. They are joined one to another, they stick together, that they cannot be sundered. By his neesings a light doth shine, and his eyes are like the eyelids of the morning. Out of his mouth go burning lamps, and sparks of fire leap out. Out of his nostrils goeth smoke, as out of a seething pot or caldron. His breath kindleth coals, and a flame goeth out of his mouth. In his neck remaineth strength, and sorrow is turned into joy before him. The flakes of his flesh are joined together: they are firm in themselves; they cannot be moved. His heart is as firm as a stone; yea, as hard as

a piece of the nether millstone. When he raiseth up himself, the mighty are afraid: by reason of breakings they purify themselves. The sword of him that layeth at him cannot hold: the spear, the dart, nor the habergeon. He esteemeth iron as straw, and brass as rotten wood. The arrow cannot make him flee: slingstones are turned with him into stubble. Darts are counted as stubble: he laugheth at the shaking of a spear. Sharp stones are under him: he spreadeth sharp pointed things upon the mire. He maketh the deep to boil like a pot: he maketh the sea like a pot of ointment. He maketh a path to shine after him; one would think the deep to be hoary. Upon earth there is not his like, who is made without fear. He beholdeth all high things: he is a king over all the children of pride.
(Job 41:1, 15-34).

The above scripture portrays the kind of satanic or demonic strongholds in the waters.   The waters have been a sort of temporary safe haven for the wicked spirits. Have you ever wondered why the unclean spirits that were cast out by Jesus Christ begged Him to send them to the

"herd of swine (that) ran violently down a steep place into the sea, and perished in the waters"? (Matthew 8:28-32).

The whole herd perished of course in the waters, but the unclean spirits did not die. The unclean spirits do not have flesh, so they cannot die; they can survive and operate from any of the realms (heavens, earth and waters). But they can be rendered ineffective by using the Word of God, the Blood and Name of Jesus Christ to bind them.

It is important to note that the way and manner the unclean spirits entered the herd of swine which led to their destruction is the same way evil spirits enter into people's lives. Most dysfunctional persons are battling with unclean spirits. The drunkards, drug addicts, hardened criminals, rebellious children and other social miscreants are victims of unclean or evil spirits afflictions. And if they are not delivered through the power of Jesus Christ, may end up destroying themselves and the unclean spirits that have been afflicting them, will find "another house" (human body to dwell). For example, Judas Iscariot that betrayed Jesus was such a victim. According to the scripture,

> *"Then entered Satan into Judas surnamed Iscariot, being of the number of the twelve." (Luke 22:3).*

And after Satan has finished using him, the bible says

> *"And he cast down the pieces of silver in the temple, and departed, and went and hanged himself." (Matthew 27:5).*

The existence of evil or unclean spirits is real, and their abode is in all the realms (heavens, earth and water). Just as we mentioned, and as you will see in subsequent chapters, people sacrifice more to the demons in the waters than to the other realms, because of the spiritual and physical import of water to the existence of man and her environment. This could explain why it takes greater spiritual efforts and sacrifices to dislodge those being held in bondage by the water spirits and their agents. In Pharaoh's Egypt it took the manifestation of ten plagues and the death of the Egyptians' first sons and livestock before Pharaoh succumbed and allowed the Israelites to embark on their journey of destiny after over four hundred years of demonic oppression and exploitation (Exodus 11:1-10, and Exodus 12:29-37).

As a result of Jesus Christ's defeat of Satan at Calvary, He re-established the dominion of man over the sea in two ways. Firstly, by a miraculous haul of fish as recorded in the gospel of Luke:

> *"Now when he had left speaking, he said unto Simon, Launch out into the deep, and let down your nets for a draught. And Simon answering said unto him, Master, we have toiled all the night, and have taken nothing: nevertheless at thy word I will let down the net. And when they had this done, they inclosed a great multitude of fishes: and their net brake"* (Luke 5:4-6).

From the above account, Jesus Christ used Peter to prove that man's dominion over the creatures of the water had been re-established. As earlier mentioned, what gave Satan the right to establish strong foundations over the creatures of the water was sin, and man lost his dominion over the fishes of the water. Peter's miraculous catch of fishes as instructed by Jesus was a testimonial that man has regained dominion over the fishes of the water:

> *"And God said, Let us make man in our image, after our likeness: and let them have dominion over the fish of the sea,... And God blessed them, and God said unto them, Be fruitful, and multiply, and replenish the earth, and subdue it: and have dominion over the fish of the sea"* *(Genesis 1:26-28).*

Secondly, when Jesus walked on the sea and invited Peter (Matthew 14:26-30), He was re-establishing man's authority over the powers of the water. According to the scripture:

"Behold, I give unto you power to tread on serpents and scorpions, and over all the power of the enemy: and nothing shall by any means hurt you."
(Luke 10:19).

Peter's walk upon the sea by invitation of Jesus Christ reconfirmed man's power and authority over the water through the Name of our Lord Jesus Christ.

This means that the powers and authorities in the waters can be subdued by man, using the Name of Jesus Christ. Because of the strongholds Satan has in the water realm, the need to be spiritually alert when dealing with marine spirits must be emphasized. The disciples know that the waters experience the activities of the spirits. That is why they assumed the night they saw Jesus

"walking on the sea... they were troubled, saying, it is a spirit... Until Jesus spake unto them, saying, Be of good cheer... And Peter answered... if it be thou, bid me come unto thee on the water. And he said, come... But when he

saw the wind boisterous, he was afraid; and began to sink, he cried, saying, Lord, save me" (Matthew 14:25-30).

The powers of the waters came after Apostle Peter through the boisterous wind. The wicked wind that came was meant to attack Peter, not Jesus Christ. Peter's faith failed him because he removed his focus from Jesus Christ.

In battle with marine powers and authorities, distraction is not permitted, because the marine spirits and powers are quite aggressive and confrontational. The demons in the water and their agents are offensive and quite courageous. And those under their oppression are held under strong bondage that is more powerful than either earth or heavenly strongholds. It is easier to deliver those under heavenly or earthly oppression than those under water because Jesus defeated the powers of the earth, and He overcame the powers of the heavenlies when he ascended to heaven. So they tremble when they hear or mention the name of Jesus Christ because victory was given at Calvary.

For those under water bondage, the deliverance is usually complex and difficult because of the covenant foundation between the water, the earth and mankind. Physically, man is a product of the earth and water. Spiritually, the Spirit of God that dwelt on the face of the water is the foundation of the breath of life that made man a living soul. So, that connection between man and the water makes our exercising complete authority over the water a daunting task. This explains the difficulties and spiritual challenges those who are in bondage of water spirits face during deliverance. Most people who are in bondage to water spirits and their agents hardly get delivered. Even when some eventually get their freedom, they are easily "re-arrested". The only way you can be set free is to be totally committed in your walk with God through Jesus Christ.

Furthermore, you must have effective spiritual cover coming under the ministration of servants of God that are anointed to destroy the works of darkness. There are different gifts and different callings. There are those who are called into deliverance ministries. Deliverance ministry is not like any other calling; God must specifically call and anoint such people for them to be effective. For example, Prophets Moses and Joshua, whom God used to deliver and take the children of Israel to the Promised Land, were both called and ordained for that purpose. Although God used Moses mightily before Pharaoh, Pharaoh did not allow Moses and the Israelites to go without strong resistance. It was the judgment of God upon him and the Egyptians that momentarily made him release the Israelites. Even when he eventually allowed them to go, Pharaoh and his cohorts still pursued the Israelites until the Red Sea consumed them.

The marine agents do not release their victims without strong deliverance; and they still do not give up trying to get their victims back. That is why most people who have been delivered from marine spirits, if they are not well grounded in prayer and the Word of God, backslide and return to their oppressors. The children of Israel told Prophet Moses as the Egyptians pursued after them:

"And when Pharaoh drew nigh, the children of Israel lifted up their eyes, and, behold, the Egyptians marched after them; and they were sore afraid... And they said unto Moses, Because there were no graves in Egypt, hast thou taken us away to die in the wilderness?... Is not this the word that we did tell thee in Egypt, saying, Let us alone, that we may serve the Egyptians?" (Exodus 14:10-12).

There are many children of God who have remained in spiritual bondage for fear of the unknown. Some have backslid and gone back because of challenging situations or circumstances they face; and they will prefer to serve "Pharaoh" because of what

"we did eat in Egypt freely; the cucumbers; and the melons, and the leeks and the onions, and the garlic (Numbers 11:4).

Some people sell their souls for the passing

pleasure of this world. They remain in bondage all the days of their life on Planet Earth.

In our time and age, the activities of the water spirits and their human agents have been on the increase. As of today, there are churches that worship goddesses of the water all over the world. In some parts of the world, voodoo devotees, white garment, red garment, green garment and blue garment church members, go to the sea, rivers or streams to perform sacrifices with animals (goats, rams, chickens, cows, etc) and pour libations of hot drinks, food and other uncooked items as gifts to the water goddesses. During such ceremonies, drums are beaten, incantations, chantings and divination practices are performed and initiations are carried out. Most of these worshippers, some out of ignorance, end up being covenanted to the water spirits, and if they are married, their children's foundation has to do with the water as well. Most people end up becoming victims of these demonic water spirits, while some become agents in the marine kingdom.

CHAPTER 3
CASE STUDIES

Some of the true stories that follow illustrate how some people come under the oppression of water spirits, and the consequences of such demonic activities.

CASE 1: CHILDLESSNESS

Mr. and Mrs. TBC were desperate to have children because they had been married for over fourteen years. They were advised that certain worship ceremonies would be performed on the seashore, and they were asked to bring some gift items and animal livestock. At midnight they joined others for the ceremonies. Precisely three months later, Mrs. TBC became pregnant and went on to have twin baby boys. But she and her husband noticed that the children behaved strangely, and kept crying all night. In the daytime they were normal, but night-times were hell.

Despite numerous deliverances and prayers, these children's development continued to be abnormal. Later in their teenage years, they became thorns in the lives of their parents. Ultimately they killed their mother, claiming that armed men had robbed and shot their parents. During the police investigation, the twins confessed to the crime. They said that over the years strange voices had spoken to them and that under their instruction, they had been held bound to a strange spirit that controlled their activities.

CASE 2: THE MURDERER

The case of a service judge in one of the states of Nigeria is almost the same. The judge had only one child, which she got after many years of trying. In her desperation to have the child she had visited a red garment church, where she had been taken to the sea for some rituals which resulted in the birth of the boy. When he was in his final year at one of the universities, he cut off his mother's head during a minor argument.

CASE 3: SUITORS CURSED WITH DEATH

Sister Bimbo Stone was the only daughter of one of the "priestesses" to the town river goddess. In her teenage years the girl refused to worship the river goddess and joined a Bible-believing fellowship centre in the school campus. After she graduated from the university and was of the age to marry, no suitor came along. This was because, whenever a man proposed to her, he died in a violent accident. She became known for such misfortune, and eventually, after many years of frustration, she committed suicide.

CASE 4: DISRUPTION IN CHURCH

In both Nigeria and in London, we have experienced some strange women who would start to confess during the services that they were marine agents sent by the powers in the water. They said they were sent to hinder the activities of the church. When the ladies were confronted, they claimed that our prayer pattern was disturbing their activities in the marine kingdom. The marine agent that manifested in London during our service was so aggressive that the church service was disrupted for over forty minutes. In fact, that case was an eye opener to some "doubting Thomases" who did not believe in the existence of marine agents. The lady began to expose her dealings in the world and how she afflicted her son, because she was not meant to have a child in this world.

CHAPTER 4

MANIFESTATIONS OF WATER/MARINE SPIRIT OPPRESSION

On a general note, as a result of our counselling experiences over the years, the following are manifestations of marine/water spirits connections or attacks:

1. PYTHON SPIRIT – SPIRIT OF DIVINATION

Satan uses this to confuse people in relation to the gift of word of knowledge/wisdom and prophecy. People from the Idemili area of Anambra State worship the python and are forbidden to kill it, since it represents the 'mother' of those from these areas.

MANIFESTATIONS

■ **Spirit Guides:** People from these areas may constantly in their dreams see two men or women acting as spiritual bodyguards and following them everywhere they go. They seem unable to shake themselves free from these 'spirit guides', even though they don't know them and don't want to be around them.

■ **Problematic Marriages:** Those with marine or python spirits tend to have problematic marriages. More women than men are possessed by marine powers, because the head of the marine kingdom is the "Queen of the Coast", who is female. Most either experience barrenness or their babies die. A friend of mine told me how her mother and all her aunts were possessed by marine spirits. One of her aunts gave birth to ten children, but four died at childbirth. Her spiritual husband would come into the ward when she was giving birth and take the child.

■ **Financial Difficulties:** Another manifestation shows in the financial and economic downturn of couples where one is possessed by marine spirits. The same aunt of my friend married a very wealthy man who began to experience great financial difficulty until he lost all he had.

■ **Sexual Immorality/High Divorce Rates:-** People from riverine areas tend to be possessed by marine spirits. This manifests as:

- Unusual sexual appetite
- High level of sexual immorality
- High divorce rates.

Since the head of the water realm is a "Queen", she cannot submit to anybody, and this is seen in women who are unable to submit to their husbands.

■ **Wicked Spirits:** They tend to be very wicked because the powers in the water are the most wicked, aggressive and confrontational.

■ **Subtlety and Deception:** Just as serpents/snakes (pythons etc) are subtle, those with the water spirit are very deceitful and deceptive. One must be very discerning to spot them.

2. NDIMIRI (MARINE PEOPLE)

In the Igbo language they are called 'Ogbanje', 'Ndi-otu' and 'Dada'. Some are initiated in the womb, especially the Ogbanje and Dada, while the Ndi-otu are initiated as children or teenagers.

■ **Ogbanje:** A lady spoke of how her mother initiated her into Ogbanje when she was still in her mother's womb. When she didn't get her way as a child, she feigned serious illness and threatened to die if her needs were not met. She used this to manipulate her parents and those around her. She became a prostitute in her teens, which is one of the requirements of Ogbanje. The idea is not necessarily to make money, but to destroy men through sexual encounters. After meeting with men who picked her up, she either changed into a python or a coffin by their side. The men later became ill with mysterious ailments and died shortly afterwards. She said that if she was in a good mood, she would just cause them to become impotent or sterile. She said sex was a powerful tool in the hands of Ogbanje, who destroy men because they hate them and want female dominion. She is now born again, thank God.

■ **Dada:** The power of the Dadas is in their hair. They do not cut or comb their hair and sometimes claim they are Nazarites. They fall sick when attempts are made to comb their hair, and if it is cut without sacrifices to the marine spirits, they die. This is a Satanic corruption of the covenant God had with Samson concerning his hair (Judges 13:5). They are usually men.

■ **Ndi-Otu:** The Ndi-Otu are usually initiated with sweets and biscuits and are both male and female. These are marine-witchcraft agents and take on the form of birds to attend their nocturnal meetings. They do this not just for ease of motion but because birds (fowls of the air) came from the water

And God said, Let the waters bring forth abundantly the moving creature that hath life, and fowl that may fly above the earth in the open firmament of heaven.

And God created great whales, and every living creature that moveth, which the waters brought forth abundantly, after their kind, and every winged fowl after his kind: and God saw that it was good. (Genesis 1:20-21:)

A young boy who lived with the woman who is now my wife (as a single lady) and her father was a member of marine witchcraft. When God exposed him, he confessed that he used to fly out by 11pm and come back between 4am and 5am when on assignment, or between 1am and 3am when he had no particular assignment. They would assemble under a tree with a pool of water. Their leader would recite an incantation and strike the water with his staff of office. The water would now open up, steps leading into the marine kingdom would appear and they would climb down. Their assignments were usually to afflict or kill the people they lived with or their family members. They also caused confusion in homes and quarrels among siblings. Divide and rule was an instrument of confusion in their hands against those they want to destroy. They used gossip, rumour and a policy of 'divide and rule' to cause division, confusion and trouble in the church. Anywhere there is scandal, shame and evil manipulation in the church, you can be sure it is the work of Ndi-Otu, marine witchcraft.

3. CONSTANT DREAMS ABOUT THE SEA OR RIVERS

Most people who see themselves by a river or sea and living a normal life there, attending ceremonies, dancing, having friends in the waters, having children, and doing normal things as if they are in the physical world, have marine connections or contacts. The need to cut off such water experiences through serious deliverance sessions cannot be over-emphasised. Some people from riverine areas experience such things because of the foundational covenant and initiation.

When I was in the world, I knew a woman who claimed she lived both in the water and on earth. People said she had married three men, who had all died in mysterious ways. After a few hourly contacts with her, I kept seeing myself in dreams living in the water. When I confronted her later, she confessed that she had a "physical spirit husband" who visited her with gifts, and that most men who went out with her died. I never saw her again after that awful encounter.

4. SEXUAL ASSAULTS IN DREAMS

Most people (both male and female) are sexually assaulted in dreams. I do not believe all sexual assaults in our sleep state are a result of water spirit connections or contacts, but when it happens on a regular basis the assumption of a spirit wife or husband relationship is reasonable. Furthermore, most people we have counselled through deliverance sessions have very similar experiences, in the following forms:

(a) Physical manifestations of sickness and tiredness all through the day.

(b) Feelings of emotional dryness and hopelessness.

(c) Feelings of alienation towards the opposite sex.

(d) Feelings of rejection, dejection, loneliness and depression.

(e) Most men who have spirit wives suffer from low sperm counts.

(f) Most women who have spirit husbands experience miscarriages.

(g) Both sexes find difficulty in finding long term partners or keeping lasting relationships

5. PROSTITUTION AND WITCHCRAFT

The water spirit is the backbone of prostitution as a profession. Most prostitutes are connected to the waters, either knowingly or unknowingly. Some women are involved in prostitution not for economic reasons but because they have a strong passion for sexual experience. This has to do with their foundations. Most children of those who practise witchcraft become victims of their parents' involvement, because the seed of witchcraft is easily transferred through sexual intercourse. This is one way to acquire an urge for prostitution and witchcraft spirits unknowingly, and most people go to the waters to be initiated so that they can effectively profit from prostitution.

Some people have confessed to using the blood of cats or pythons for initiation in the waters, to give them the ability to arouse or excite the opposite sex into doing their bidding.

6. SOUL-TIES

Those who cannot stop thinking of former relationships, even when they are married or spiritually separated, are suffering from water spirit afflictions. Their minds are being bombarded with obscene thoughts about those relationships. We have counselled men and women who have good marital relations, but cannot stop thinking about 'old flames'. Some people cannot even enjoy intimate relations with their partners unless they recall the carnal activities of past relationships. It is mainly single parents who have to deal with such issues, and if they are not checked through deliverance intervention, their children end up damaged.

The problem is then handed down from generation to generation.

7. ABORTION

The demonic powers and authorities in the water love the blood of little children. That is the reason why Pharaoh commanded that the male children of Israel should be sacrificed to the water gods of the River Nile. Most young girls who have abortions are controlled by the water spirits. We have counselled a young lady who would deliberately allow herself to become pregnant, with no intention of having a child, but just so that she could have an abortion. She confessed that her "spirit husband" encouraged her and that she would never have peace until she aborted the child. She said the abortion was usually carried out before the third month of the pregnancy. This continued even after she was married. After much pressure she told her husband the real story of her experiences, and she was brought for deliverance. After some weeks of prayers and fasting sessions, she overcame the powers of darkness that were controlling her life.

8. NEAR-SUCCESS SYNDROME, OR MISFORTUNE THROUGH REJECTION

Some people complain of never feeling loved, and being constantly rejected. Even when they show kindness to other people, they are rewarded with insults or misfortune. Most often, from our experiences, these are projections from the water realm. According to the confession of a former witch doctor who is now a Minister of God, these wicked and deadly acts can be brought about by writing a person's name on a sheet of paper, then spraying a lizard's blood on the paper and putting it into a bottle. After pronouncing some dark sayings through enchantment into the bottle, it is thrown into a river or the sea. The victim will never experience favour or kindness from people.

The witch doctor told us that most mothers-in-law indulge in such wicked practices against their daughters-in-law. In fact most people whose foundation has to do with the waters have the same experiences. This is because the demonic powers and authorities in the waters eventually afflict those who work for them. Again, this is because those who serve and worship Satan often generate a negative aura around them.

I have noticed that none of my primary and secondary schoolmates whose fathers were involved in water spirit worship and practice prospered in life. As the Psalmist said:

"I have been young, and now am old; yet have I not seen the righteous forsaken, nor his seed begging bread?"
(Psalms 37:25).

Conversely, for the unrighteous who work for Satanic powers, they and their seed will never experience favour or excel in their endeavours.

CHAPTER 5

SUMMARY

The problems of most people who experience extreme abuse, alienation, alcoholism, materialism, addictions, criminal activities and other neurotic and psychotic behaviours and tendencies are rooted in the activities of the powers and authorities in the waters. That is why the scriptures say that Jesus Christ came to undo the works of darkness in all realms. The fact that Jesus Christ walked on the face of the waters was essentially to demonstrate that He has dominion over the powers, principalities, thrones and authorities of the waters. Because

"God has given Him a name which is above every other name: that at the name of Jesus, every knee should bow, of things in heaven, and things in the earth, and things under the earth" – the waters (Philippians 2:9-10).

And since water is under the earth, those who are in bondage of the water demonic forces can destroy the foundations of their bondages by utilising the sword of the spirit (Ephesians 6:17). The Word of God is the sword you can use to demolish Satanic strongholds, strong men and women, covens and roots of afflictions in your life through undertaking these prophetic prayer points.

The combination of the Word of God and the Name of Jesus Christ in your personal challenges will avail many victories, promotions and breakthroughs. As a child of God, this is the time to bind and paralyse forces in the water holding you down from possessing your God-given possessions in Jesus' Name. As you embark on these prayer sessions, your time to do exploits has just begun and no power or authority in the waters can stop you, in Jesus' Name, Amen.

Enter into the realm of prayers as you open the next chapter.

CHAPTER 6 - PRAYER POINTS

CONFESSIONS

Confession of sins is very important before going to God in prayers, because sin can prevent our prayers from being answered. In Romans 3:23, the Bible says: *"For all have sinned, and come short of the glory of God"*; It is therefore imperative to confess every known and unknown sin as we come to God in prayers.

1

Isaiah 59:1-2

Behold, the LORD's hand is not shortened, that it cannot save; neither his ear heavy, that it cannot hear: But your iniquities have separated between you and your God, and your sins have hid his face from you, that he will not hear

O Lord my God, I confess all my sins and ask for your forgiveness and cleanse me from all unrighteousness in Jesus' Name, Amen.

2

Revelation 12:11

And they overcame him by the blood of the Lamb, and by the word of their testimony; and they loved not their lives unto the death.

O Lord my God, I cover myself in the blood of Jesus Christ and I confess that the blood of Jesus Christ has rendered powerless Water/Marine strongholds in my life in Jesus Name, Amen.

FOUNDATIONS

Your foundation is very important to how far you can go in life. Some people's foundations are linked to water/marine spirits, eg those whose parents are marine native doctors, or attend white garment churches, or have relationship with those with marine connections, and those who live in the riverine areas. This ungodly foundation can hinder their spiritual lives, progress and marital relationships, to mention but these. That is why the bible says in Psalm 11:3: *"If the foundations be destroyed, what can the righteous do?"* It is therefore essential to begin this prayer exercise by dealing with foundational issues.

3

2 Corinthians 6:17:

Wherefore come out from among them, and be ye separate, saith the Lord, and touch not the unclean thing; and I will receive you.

O Lord my God, I use the Blood of Jesus Christ to separate myself from every marine or water covenants or initiations, in Jesus' Name, Amen.

4 *Psalms 11:3*

If the foundations be destroyed, what can the righteous do?

O Lord my God, every marine or water connections or contacts in my foundation, be destroyed in Jesus' Name, Amen.

5 *Numbers 23:1:*

And Balaam said unto Balak, Build me here seven altars, and prepare me here seven oxen and seven rams.

O Lord my God, every marine or water altar erected in my foundations be destroyed by the Holy Ghost Fire in Jesus' Name, Amen.

6 *1 Corinthians 10:20:*

But I say, that the things which the Gentiles sacrifice, they sacrifice to devils, and not to God: and I would not that ye should have fellowship with devils.

O Lord my God, I use the Blood of Jesus Christ to cancel blood sacrifices made to the powers in the water on my behalf, in Jesus' Name, Amen.

7 *1 Kings 11:8:*

And likewise did he for all his strange wives, which burnt incense and sacrificed unto their gods.

O Lord my God, I use the Blood of Jesus Christ to cancel every incense and blood sacrifice made to water spirits by my forefathers, parents, relatives, husband or wife, in Jesus' Name, Amen.

BINDING AND RELEASING

God wants us to prosper, but some of us are not prospering because the evil ones are fighting against our blessings. Before our blessings can be released and come to us, we must first of all bind those evil powers hindering them. That is why Jesus said in Matthew 12:29: *"Or else how can one enter into a strong man's house, and spoil his goods, except he first bind the strong man? and then he will spoil his house."* The ability to bind and release is a very powerful privilege of every child of God. In Matthew 18:18, Jesus said: *"Verily I say unto you, Whatsoever ye shall bind on earth shall be bound in heaven: and whatsoever ye shall loose on earth shall be loosed in heaven."*

8 Matthew 18:18: *Verily I say unto you, Whatsoever ye shall bind on earth shall be bound in heaven: and whatsoever ye shall loose on earth shall be loosed in heaven.*

O Lord my God, I use the Blood of Jesus Christ to bind and paralyse water spirits assigned against me, in Jesus' Name, Amen.

9

Or else how can one enter into a strong man's house, and spoil his goods, except he first bind the strong man? and then he will spoil his house.

O Lord my God, you marine strongman or woman in my life, I use the Blood of Jesus Christ to bind and paralyse you, in Jesus' Name, Amen.

10

And his feet like unto fine brass, as if they burned in a furnace; and his voice as the sound of many waters.

O Lord my God, I use the Blood of Jesus Christ to silence the sound of voices in the water speaking against my blessings, in Jesus' Name, Amen.

11

And there came one of the seven angels which had the seven vials, and talked with me, saying unto me, Come hither; I will shew unto thee the judgment of the great whore that sitteth upon many waters: With whom the kings of the earth have committed fornication, and the inhabitants of the earth have been made drunk with the wine of her fornication.

O Lord my God, any man or woman who operates with the spirit of lust from the water, assigned to destroy me, I bind you in Jesus' Name, Amen.

12 *Numbers 23:23:* *Surely there is no enchantment against Jacob, neither is there any divination against Israel: according to this time it shall be said of Jacob and of Israel, What hath God wrought!*

O Lord my God, I use the Blood of Jesus Christ to bind and paralyse marine enchantments and divinations targeted at me in Jesus' Name, Amen.

13 *Proverbs 8:29:* *When he gave to the sea his decree, that the waters should not pass his commandment: when he appointed the foundations of the earth.*

O Lord my God, I use the Blood of Jesus Christ to cancel all decrees to the powers and authorities in the sea meant to hinder or afflict me, in Jesus' Name, Amen.

14 *Isaiah 11:15:* *And the LORD shall utterly destroy the tongue of the Egyptian sea; and with his mighty wind shall he shake his hand over the river, and shall smite it in the seven streams, and make men go over dryshod.*

O Lord my God, I use the Blood of Jesus Christ to cancel all decrees to the powers and authorities in the sea meant to hinder or afflict me, in Jesus' Name, Amen.

15 *Then all the princes of the sea shall come down from their thrones, and lay away their robes, and put off their broidered garments: they shall clothe themselves with trembling; they shall sit upon the ground, and shall tremble at every moment, and be astonished at thee.*

Ezekiel 26:16:

O Lord my God, all the princes of the sea assigned against me be paralysed in Jesus' Name, Amen.

16 *And four great beasts came up from the sea, diverse one from another.*

Daniel 7:3:

O Lord my God, great beasts in the seas or waters meant to hinder me be paralysed in Jesus' Name, Amen.

17 *Seek him that maketh the seven stars and Orion, and turneth the shadow of death into the morning, and maketh the day dark with night: that calleth for the waters of the sea, and poureth them out upon the face of the earth: The LORD is his name.*

Amos 5:8:

O Lord my God, any man or woman who will call upon the waters of the seas in order to afflict me, will not live to execute their evil imaginations in Jesus' Name, Amen.

18

Psalm 144:7:

Send thine hand from above; rid me, and deliver me out of great waters, from the hand of strange children.

O Lord my God, I loose myself from the traps of many waters, in Jesus' Name, Amen.

19

Psalm 106:9:

He rebuked the Red sea also, and it was dried up: so he led them through the depths, as through the wilderness.

O Lord my God, I rebuke the powers and authorities in the seas, assigned against me, in Jesus' Name, Amen.

20

Job 27:20:

Terrors take hold on him as waters, a tempest stealeth him away in the night.

O Lord my God, terrors in the waters assigned against me be paralysed in Jesus' Name, Amen..

21

Psalm 74:13:

Thou didst divide the sea by thy strength: thou brakest the heads of the dragons in the waters.

O Lord my God, I use the Blood of Jesus Christ to bind and paralyse head of dragons in the water, assigned against me, in Jesus' Name, Amen.

22 *Behold, the LORD will cast her out, and he will smite her power in the sea; and she shall be devoured with fire.*

Zechariah 9:4:

O Lord my God, powers in the seas hindering my blessings, be rendered powerless in Jesus' Name, Amen.

23 *And he saith unto them, Why are ye fearful, O ye of little faith? Then he arose, and rebuked the winds and the sea; and there was a great calm.*

Matthew 8:26:

O Lord my God, I use the Blood of Jesus Christ to rebuke demonic powers in the wind and sea working together in order to frustrate me, in Jesus' Name, Amen.

24 *And Hiram sent in the navy his servants, shipmen that had knowledge of the sea, with the servants of Solomon.*

1 Kings 9:27:

O Lord my God, any man or woman using the secret knowledge of the sea against me, be paralysed in Jesus' Name, Amen.

25 *Behold, they shall surely gather together, but not by me: whosoever shall gather together against thee shall fall for thy sake.*

Isaiah 54:15:

O Lord my God, whenever those who utilise the services of the powers of the seas will gather against me, I command confusion to come upon them in Jesus' Name, Amen.

26 *And when it was day, certain of the Jews banded together, and bound themselves under a curse, saying that they would neither eat nor drink till they had killed Paul.*

O Lord my God, whenever a group of men or women or both gather in the waters with evil vows or oaths fashioned against me, let them harvest their dark utterances in Jesus' Name, Amen.

27 *Thou shalt bring them in, and plant them in the mountain of thine inheritance, in the place, O LORD, which thou hast made for thee to dwell in, in the Sanctuary, O LORD, which thy hands have established.*

O Lord my God, any group of men or women or both who will ever encamp by the waters naked in order to afflict me, they shall never live to execute their evil plans in Jesus' Name, Amen.

28 *And I stood upon the sand of the sea, and saw a beast rise up out of the sea, having seven heads and ten horns, and upon his horns ten crowns, and upon his heads the name of blasphemy.*

O Lord my God, every gathering of the beasts of the seas against me, is scattered in Jesus' Name, Amen.

29

Jeremiah 1:13:

And the word of the LORD came unto me the second time, saying, What seest thou? And I said, I see a seething pot; and the face thereof is toward the north.

O Lord my God, every demonic pot or pots buried in the waters meant to hinder my blessings, be destroyed in Jesus' Name, Amen.

30

Isaiah 44:25:

That frustrateth the tokens of the liars, and maketh diviners mad; that turneth wise men backward, and maketh their knowledge foolish;

O Lord my God, whoever has gone to the waters or seas to call my names for evil, shame, accident, failure, sickness or death, they will harvest their dark imaginations in Jesus' Name, Amen.

31

Matthew 16:18:

And I say also unto thee, That thou art Peter, and upon this rock I will build my church; and the gates of hell shall not prevail against it.

O Lord my God, gates of hell in the waters, erected to hinder my finances, health, marriage and blessings, be destroyed by Holy Ghost fire in Jesus' Name, Amen.

DECREE AND DECLARE

As we did mention, the spirit realm is governed by decrees and commands. The Water Realm, like any other creation of God, has the ability to obey commands and carry out instructions. All through the bible, God, and even men of God, issued commands to the Water to do their will. In the same manner, we are to command the Water to obey us in order to accomplish our purposes. In Job 22:28, the bible says: *"Thou shalt also decree a thing, and it shall be established unto thee: and the light shall shine upon thy ways."*

32 *Genesis 1:26:* *And God said, Let us make man in our image, after our likeness: and let them have dominion over the fish of the sea, and over the fowl of the air, and over the cattle, and over all the earth, and over every creeping thing that creepeth upon the earth.*

O Lord my God, I decree and declare that I have dominion over the creatures of the seas in Jesus' Name, Amen.

33 *He shall have dominion also from sea to sea, and from the river unto the ends of the earth.*

Psalm 72:8:

O Lord my God, I decree and declare that I have dominion over the powers and authorities of the seas in Jesus' Name, Amen.

34 *And he saith unto them, Why are ye fearful, O ye of little faith? Then he arose, and rebuked the winds and the sea; and there was a great calm.*

Matthew 8:26:

O Lord my God, I decree and declare that demonic powers and authorities in the seas assigned against me be paralysed in Jesus' Name, Amen.

35 *The LORD on high is mightier than the noise of many waters, yea, than the mighty waves of the sea.*

Psalm 93:4:

O Lord my God, I decree and declare that voices on many waters in the seas speaking against my blessings be silenced in Jesus' Name, Amen.

36 *For this is as the waters of Noah unto me: for as I have sworn that the waters of Noah should no more go over the earth; so have I sworn that I would not be wroth with thee, nor rebuke thee.*

Isaiah 54:9:

O Lord my God, I decree and declare that the waters of Noah will never near my dwelling place in Jesus' Name, Amen.

37 *And they shall wander from sea to sea, and from the north even to the east, they shall run to and fro to seek the word of the LORD, and shall not find it.*

Amos 8:12:

O Lord my God, I decree and declare that all those using marine powers to fight me, will wander from seas to sea in Jesus' Name, Amen.

38 *Be thou ashamed, O Zidon: for the sea hath spoken, even the strength of the sea, saying, I travail not, nor bring forth children, neither do I nourish up young men, nor bring up virgins.*

Isaiah 23:4:

O Lord my God, I decree and declare that every dark spoken word of the seas against me is hereby cancelled by the Blood of Jesus Christ, Amen.

39 *And he led them on safely, so that they feared not: but the sea overwhelmed their enemies.*

Psalm 78:53:

O Lord my God, I decree and declare that as those who hate me come to the sea to curse me, let the sea overwhelm them in Jesus' Name, Amen.

40 *Which made heaven, and earth, the sea, and all that therein is: which keepeth truth for ever.*

Psalm 146:6:

O Lord my God, I decree and declare, let the sea and all that is therein fight my battles in Jesus' Name, Amen.

41 *The sacrifice of the wicked is an abomination to the LORD: but the prayer of the upright is his delight.*

Proverbs 15:8:

O Lord my God, I decree and declare that the sacrifices of the wicked to the powers and authorities in the waters meant to afflict me, be rendered null and void in Jesus' Name, Amen.

42 *Canst thou lift up thy voice to the clouds, that abundance of waters may cover thee?*

Job 38:34:

O Lord and God, I decree and declare that the abundance of the water is my portion in Jesus' Name, Amen.

43 *He maketh me to lie down in green pastures: he leadeth me beside the still waters.*

Psalm 23:2:

O Lord my God, I decree and declare that God will lead me beside the still waters in Jesus' Name, Amen.

44 *And Moses stretched forth his hand over the sea, and the sea returned to his strength when the morning appeared; and the Egyptians fled against it; and the LORD overthrew the Egyptians in the midst of the sea.*

Exodus 14:27:

O Lord my God, I decree and declare that evil men and women in the midst of the sea invoking my name, have been overthrown by God in Jesus' Name, Amen.

45 | Isaiah 28:17:

Judgment also will I lay to the line, and righteousness to the plummet: and the hail shall sweep away the refuge of lies, and the waters shall overflow the hiding place.

O Lord my God, I decree and declare that the waters will overflow and destroy the hiding place of the wicked assigned against me in Jesus' Name, Amen.

46 | Psalm 46:3:

Though the waters thereof roar and be troubled, though the mountains shake with the swelling thereof.

O Lord my God, I decree and declare that the roaring of the waters against my blessings and promotion have ceased in Jesus' Name, Amen.

47 | 2 Kings 18:31:

Hearken not to Hezekiah: for thus saith the king of Assyria, Make an agreement with me by a present, and come out to me, and then eat ye every man of his own vine, and every one of his fig tree, and drink ye every one the waters of his cistern.

O Lord my God, I decree and declare that satanic water pots or cisterns that the marine powers and authorities are using against me, are hereby destroyed in Jesus' Name, Amen.

48

Unstable as water, thou shalt not excel; because thou wentest up to thy father's bed; then defiledst thou it: he went up to my couch.

O Lord my God, I decree and declare that my business, marriage, children and beloved ones, will never be unstable as the water in Jesus' Name, Amen.

49

And with the blast of thy nostrils the waters were gathered together, the floods stood upright as an heap, and the depths were congealed in the heart of the sea.

O Lord my God, I decree and declare that satanic or demonic secrets congealed in the heart of the sea, meant to hinder my blessings, are hereby exposed in Jesus' Name, Amen.

50

O thou that dwellest upon many waters, abundant in treasures, thine end is come, and the measure of thy covetousness.

O Lord my God, I decree and declare that powers and authorities dwelling upon many waters assigned against me have been paralysed in Jesus' Name, Amen.

51 *Let them melt away as waters which run continually: when he bendeth his bow to shoot his arrows, let them be as cut in pieces.*

O Lord my God, I thank you for answered prayers and my enemies have all melted away as waters in Jesus' Name, Amen.

NOTES

NOTES

NOTES

Made in United States
Troutdale, OR
05/19/2024